The Perfect Storm of 1991: The Story of the Nor'easter that Sank the *Andrea Gail*

By Charles River Editors

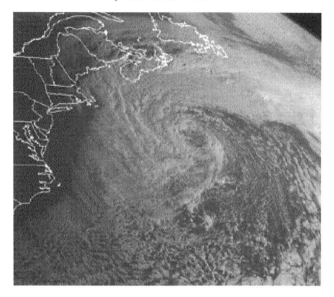

Satellite image of the storm on October 30, 1991

About Charles River Editors

Charles River Editors provides superior editing and original writing services across the digital publishing industry, with the expertise to create digital content for publishers across a vast range of subject matter. In addition to providing original digital content for third party publishers, we also republish civilization's greatest literary works, bringing them to new generations of readers via ebooks.

Sign up here to receive updates about free books as we publish them, and visit Our Kindle Author Page to browse today's free promotions and our most recently published Kindle titles.

Introduction

Satellite image of the storm over Nova Scotia on November 2, 1991

The Perfect Storm of 1991 (October-November 1991)

"The technical name for the new storm was a 'midlatitude cyclone.' The people in its path, however, would later call it the No Name Hurricane, since it had all the force of a hurricane, but was never officially designated as one. And because the brunt of the storm would strike the eastern seaboard around October 31, it would also acquire another name: the Halloween Gale." – Sebastian Junger, author of *The Perfect Storm*

People in the Northeastern United States have been dealing with winter storms for centuries, band people in the South and on the East Coast have dealt with hurricanes and tropical storms for just as long, but it's rare for the weather systems that produce such storms to actually collide with each other and produce a more powerful storm. In fact, it's unusual enough that when it happened in late October 1991, one weatherman dubbed it the "Perfect Storm."

Indeed, the Perfect Storm of 1991 was unique in many respects. By feeding off of Hurricane Grace and another storm to the south, the Nor'easter that was hitting the Northeast and Canada became an incredibly powerful storm that struck the North Atlantic before swinging back south and again developing into a tropical storm. In the process, it produced waves in excess of 100 feet tall near Nova Scotia and caused substantial flooding across the East Coast. It was also responsible for a handful of deaths throughout the region.

The storm may have been one of those that residents in the area would remember and talk about in comparison to subsequent storms, but the Perfect Storm is well-known across the country thanks to Sebastian Junger's book, *The Perfect Storm*. In 2000, the movie *The Perfect Storm* dramatized Junger's book and the true story of the sinking of the *Andrea Gail*, a fishing ship based out of Gloucester, Massachusetts that got caught up in the storm and sank with all hands on board. Although there were other dramatic events that took place in relation to the storm, including the rescue of the crew of a downed helicopter in the midst of the storm, the tragedy of the *Andrea Gail* continues to provide the most human face to the infamous storm.

The Perfect Storm of 1991: The Story of the Nor'easter that Sank the Andrea Gail chronicles the storm from its formation to the devastating effects it had across the Atlantic. Along with pictures and a bibliography, you will learn about the Perfect Storm like never before, in no time at all.

The Perfect Storm of 1991: The Story of the Nor'easter that Sank the *Andrea Gail*

About Charles River Editors

Introduction

Chapter 1: Not Expected to Pose a Serious Threat

"Hurricane Grace churned today across the Atlantic Ocean, hundreds of miles away from land. Forecasters said that the tropical storm that surged to hurricane strength late Sunday was not expected to pose a serious threat to land as it moved northwest at about 9 mph. 'We think it'll turn well before it reaches the U.S.,' said hurricane specialist Hal Gerrish at the National Hurricane Center in suburban Coral Gables. 'It's still over warm water, but it looks like the steering currents are going to take it into an area where conditions will not be favorable for strengthening.' Gerrish said. … The only possible effect expected on the East Coast was increasing swells in waters along the East Coast and possible erosion, said the forecasters." - *The Index-Journal* (Greenwood, South Carolina), Monday, October 28, 1991, Page 1-2

Someone once observed that "everybody talks about the weather but no one ever does anything about it." This is a fair observation, given that people cannot control the water but only predict it with varying degrees of accuracy and prepare to handle it with varying degrees of success. At the same time, people tend to become blasé about any kind of weather that their part of the country experiences. People in Alaska don't mind the cold, people in Arizona handle the heat, and people in the Northeast tend to be less frightened by the idea of a blizzard or a Nor'easter than those living further south, who frequently deal with low category hurricanes.

Thus, it is no surprise that, on Sunday morning, October 27, 1991, the people of Bermuda were enjoying the rare pleasure of having an extra hour of sleep thanks to the clocks turning back an hour. When people finally did wake up, they noted with only passing interest that the weather was looking nasty and that it seemed that the mild tropical storm, Grace, was going to kick up some wind and rain as she passed by that evening. Bermuda is an island accustomed to tropical storms, including ones much stronger than Grace, so people took their usual precautions but were otherwise unconcerned. As Miles Lawrence, a weather forecaster in the area, noted, "The wind just hadn't been high enough that you'd expect any damage other than some tree limbs and stuff." Little did they realize, as the rain fell, that they had the dubious honor of being the first to experience what would soon be known as the "Perfect Storm."

When the people of Bermuda woke up the next morning, they learned that the once little tropical storm Grace had grown up overnight. According to one story out of the Associated Press, "A hurricane warning was posted Monday for Bermuda as Hurricane Grace with winds of near 75 mph, took an eastward turn away from the U.S. mainland and threatened the island. Bands of showers and squalls swept Bermuda throughout the day, and hurricane conditions were possible by early Tuesday…the storm's track was wobbling because of a winter storm near Nova Scotia. 'The hurricane is trying to go around the storm,' said forecaster Jack Bevin. 'The winter storm will become the predominant weather system and may eventually destroy the hurricane.'"

Satellite image of Hurricane Grace on October 28

Bevin's prediction proved to be partially correct, but while the Nor'easter out of Nova Scotia did prove to be the bigger storm, it did not destroy Hurricane Grace so much as join it. Elizabeth Bernier was living in Massachusetts at the time and witnessed their union, as well as the results, firsthand. She later wrote, "I was renting a house on the ocean, literally a few feet from the water. I had been packed up and readied for a move back to my own home, a mile inland. My moving date was delayed because the tenants living in the house I owned were also delayed in moving out. The storm had been building for a couple of days. On Monday, October 28, I recall hearing sirens as I was driving out of my street to go to work. Police and fire trucks screamed down Gannett Road in front of me and came to a halt at the water's edge. The police and firemen then appeared to look helplessly out to sea, watching a sailboat that seemed ready to founder onto the rocks off Minot Ledge, a half mile off shore. The sea was very stormy that morning."

By the time Hurricane Grace joined the Nor'easter, however, the two were not alone. A third storm, spawned by a weather system that originally broke off from Grace, had hit the cold air coming down from Canada and grown into an independent storm in its own right before converging with the Nor'easter and causing the highest waves ever measured in Nova Scotia.

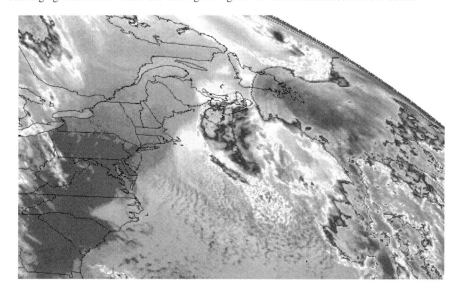

A satellite image of the storms combining over the Atlantic on October 29

Chapter 2: Developing Storm

"Six young men set out on a dead-calm sea to seek their fortunes. Suddenly they were hit by the worst gale in a century, and there wasn't even time to shout." – Sebastian Junger, "The Storm"

Ironically, the most famous story to come out of the "Perfect Storm" started before the storm developed and ended before the storm petered out in the Atlantic. Within weeks of the last wave crashing ashore, Sebastian Junger, a freelance journalist, began work on his most famous book to date, *The Perfect Storm*. In the book, Junger detailed many stories that occurred during the storm, but the one that captured the imaginations of most of his readers and led to a Hollywood movie by the same name was that of the *Andrea Gail*, which sailed from Gloucester, Massachusetts on September 27 on what became her last fishing trip. Junger described the fishing vessel in a 1994 article: "The *Andrea Gail* was one of maybe a dozen big commercial boats gearing up in Gloucester in mid-September 1991. She was owned by Bob Brown, a longtime fisherman who was known locally as Suicide Brown because of the risks he'd taken as a young man. He owned a second long liner, the *Hannah Boden*, and a couple of lobster boats. The *Andrea Gail* and the *Hannah Boden* were Brown's biggest investments, collectively worth well over a million dollars. The *Andrea Gail*, in the language, was a raked-stem, hard-chinned, western-rig boat. That meant that her bow had a lot of angle to it, she had a nearly square cross-section, and her pilothouse was up front rather than in the stern. She was built of welded steel plate, rust-red below waterline, green above, and she had a white wheelhouse with half-inch-thick safety glass windows. Fully rigged, for a long trip, she carried hundreds of miles of monofilament line, thousands of hooks, and 10,000 pounds of baitfish. There were seven life preservers on board, six survival suits, an emergency position indicating radio beacon, and one life raft."

Justin Hoch's picture of Tim Hetherington (left) and Sebastian Junger in 2011

On October 25, days before Hurricane Grace was a concern to anyone, the captain of the *Andrea Gail*, Billy Tyne, set sail for home, hoping to outrun the Nor'easter that was just beginning to brew. Junger described Tyne as "a former carpenter and drug counselor who had switched to fishing at age 27. Tyne had a reputation as a fearless captain, and in his ten years of professional fishing he had made it through several treacherous storms. Junger also noted, "Jobs aboard Tyne's boat were sought after." In part, that track record ultimately worked against the crew, because as a veteran of fishing and bad weather, Tyne was no more concerned about the coming weather than anyone else was.

Tragically, Tyne and his five man crew soon learned that they were dealing with something far worse than anything they had ever experienced before, a point driven home by the warnings issued on October 27. Junger explained, "The *Andrea Gail* had been out 38 days when the National Weather Service suddenly started issuing fax bulletins about a low-pressure system that was building over southern Quebec and heading out to sea: 'DEVELOPING STORM 45N 73W MOVING E 24 KTS. WINDS INCREASING TO 35 KTS AND SEAS BUILDING TO 16 FT.' Meanwhile, the Weather Service was keeping a close eye on the mid-Atlantic, where Hurricane Grace, which had developed in the vicinity of Bermuda two days before, was now tracking steadily northwest toward the Carolina coast. It was Sunday, October 27, very late to be pushing one's luck on the Grand Banks. Most of the fleet was well to the east of Tyne, out on the high seas, but a 150-foot Japanese sword boat named the Eishan Maru and the 77-foot Mary T were fishing nearby. Tyne told Albert Johnston, the Mary T's captain, that he had 40,000 pounds of fish in his hold - an impressive catch - and now he was heading home." – Sebastian Junger, "The Storm"

However, on October 28, while sailing off the coast of Nova Scotia, the *Andrea Gail* ran headlong into the as yet unnamed storm that had formed when the other three storms combined. That evening, around 6:00, Tyne radioed Linda Greenlaw, captain of the *Andrea Gail*'s sister ship, the *Hannah Boden*, that he estimated the wind to be blowing between 50-80 miles per hour. A few minutes later, he radioed again, crying out, "She's comin' on, boys, and she's comin' on strong." This was the last message any other boat received from the *Andrea Gail*. At some point during the next few hours, the ship went down, likely swamped by waves in excess of 60 feet high.

Though no one could know with any certainty what actually happened, Junger put together a likely scenario based on his research: "She was probably running with the waves and slightly angled toward them– 'quartering down-sea,' as it's called–which is a stable position for a boat; she'll neither plow her nose into the sea nor roll over broadside. A wave must be bigger than a boat to flip her end-over-end, and the Andrea Gail was 70 feet long. But by this point, data buoys off Nova Scotia were measuring waves as high as 100 feet–among the highest readings ever recorded. Near Sable Island the troughs of such monsters would have reached the ocean floor. Tyne would have radioed for help if trouble had come on slowly–a leak or a gradual foundering, for example. 'Whatever happened, happened quick,' a former crew member from the Hannah Boden later said. Tyne didn't even have time to grab the radio and shout. When the rogue hit the Andrea Gail, sometime between midnight and dawn on October 29, Tyne would probably have been alone in the wheelhouse and already exhausted after 24 hours at the helm. … The crew would have been below deck, either in the kitchen or in their staterooms. Once in a while one of the men would have come up to keep Tyne company. In the privacy of the wheelhouse he might have admitted his fears: This is bad, this is the worst I've ever seen. There's no way we could inflate a life raft in these conditions. If a hatch breaks open, if anything lets go…"

Meanwhile, the weather was only getting worse and the waves higher. Some of the men may have prayed, and others may thought about loved ones, but Tyne likely carried on, just as a captain in charge of the lives of others typically does. Junger's vivid theory of how the ship likely sank paints an ugly picture: "Tyne must have looked back and seen an exceptionally big wave rising up behind him. It would have been at least 70 feet high, maybe 100 feet. The stern of the boat would have risen up sickeningly and hurled the men from their bunks. The Andrea Gail would have flipped end-over-end and landed hull-up, exploding the wheelhouse windows. Tyne, upside-down in his steel cage, would have drowned without a word. The five men below deck would have landed on the ceiling. The ones who remained conscious would have known that it was impossible to escape through an open hatch and swim out from under the boat. And even if they could - what then? How would they have found their survival suits, the life raft? The Andrea Gail would have rolled drunkenly and started to fill. Water would have sprayed through bursting gaskets and risen in a column from the wheelhouse stairway. It would have reached the men in their staterooms and it would have been cold enough to take their breath away. At least the end would have come fast."

For her part, Greenlaw later discussed her far less dramatic experiences during the storm: "Readers of *The Perfect Storm* are curious about my experience in the Halloween gale, and are often disappointed when I explain to them that where I was located the weather was not life-threatening. This is not to downplay the severity of the storm. I knew how bad it was when I saw the wreckage it left in its wake. I lost six friends in that storm. But I was 600 miles east of where the *Andrea Gail* is believed to have gone down, and 400 miles east of where the 100-foot waves were recorded. I would be lying if I said that my crew and I were never concerned for our own safety during that storm. We were in radio contact with the men west of us whose lives were in danger, and something in their voices scared us deeply. Fortunately for us, though, by the time the storm reached our position, it had diminished to a state somewhat less than perfect. We encountered 70 knots of wind for two days; this was truly miserable, but by no means the worst winds we had ever seen."

Likewise, Ethel Shatford, whom Junger later described as, "a strong, gray-faced Gloucester native in her late fifties," discussed her last encounter with four of the men on the *Andrea Gail*: "The Andrea Gail crew left from this bar. They were all standing over there by the pool table saying good-bye. About the only thing different that time was that Billy Tyne let them take our color TV on the boat. He said, 'Ethel, they can take the TV, but if they watch it instead of doing their work, the TV's going overboard.' I said, That's fine, Billy, that's fine."

Chapter 3: A Yellow Tinge

"At 2:00 p.m. I finished with my last client and went upstairs to the main floor to get some lunch. I had one remaining appointment at 6:30 p.m. By this time the white surf had developed a yellow tinge and the froth was covering the entire front window wall of the house which was made of sliding glass doors and floor-to-ceiling glass panels. With each wave hitting the seawall, the white foam slapped against the windows, completely covering the view from top to bottom and side to side. Then, very slowly, the froth would slide down the windows to reveal the sea again until, in a few seconds, the next wave would hit and the froth would slap the windows, obliterating the view. It seemed to be the consistency of shaving cream, very thick and very slow to slide down the window glass." - Elizabeth Bernier

Though the crew of the *Andrea Gail* were likely lost by Tuesday morning, October 29, the weather was just beginning to make its presence felt on the shores of New England. Elizabeth Bernier recalled, "On Tuesday, I took note of the solid whiteness of the water from the shoreline, extending eastward, out to the horizon and as far as I could see, up and down the coastline. I had never seen anything like it before; no hint of darker water between waves to separate the foam of the caps. As far as the eye could see, the scene was a solid sheet of white caps. That scene continues to puzzle me. Tuesday night when I returned home from work, I turned on my all-weather radio to check on the storm's progress. It was reported that high tide on Wednesday would be at 4:15 a.m. and then again at 4:30 p.m. and that two storm systems were converging to create a sizeable high tide with potential flooding in low-lying areas. A storm out of Canada was coming south and east into New England while the tail end of the latest hurricane had moved out to sea but was joining in the Canadian air coming from the northeast."

Seasoned shore dwellers knew that the worst time for a storm to hit is when the tide was coming in, so they began to prepare for the onslaught. Bernier continued, "Having heard that report, I was somewhat prepared for what happened during the night. Ordinarily, a storm at sea that creates large surf shakes the house when high tide pounds the seawall. I had quickly become accustomed to this phenomena within a month of living there. However, I was suddenly and violently awakened at 2:00 a.m. by crashing waves on the seawall, rocking the house with such fury I thought it was coming off its foundation. I flew out of my bed, which was located on the third floor, and ran down to the second floor living room to assess the danger. I decided to get ready in the event I would need to leave quickly. I dressed accordingly, and put my sleeping bag on the living room couch, my purse near the stairs leading to the first floor door where my car was parked. I tried in vain to sleep but ended up sitting in my rocking chair watching the fury of the tide coming in for the next two to three hours."

Bernier was not the only person awakened by the storm's ferocity that night. As the winds and the waves beat against houses and land, trees fell and water rose. Still, most people remained calm and hoped daybreak would bring better weather. Bernier remembered, "I recall only a moment of fear during that time. When my eyes had adjusted to the dark, I could perceive an enormous wave approaching from about half way out on the horizon. The thought of a tidal wave flashed through my mind and I wondered if this could be one! Slowly, I saw the same size wave repeated and decided it couldn't be tidal — just extremely high surf rolling in, crashing over the seawall. I watched as the waves traveled over the seawall, crashing between my house and the one next door — water rolling down the concrete stairs that led from the concrete apron to the back yard and flooding the street. I saw my son's ladder being swept by the water to the neighbor's lawn across the road. The street was filled with water, white froth and debris. At this point I remember noting that someone was at the house next door, as I could see TV lights in an upstairs bedroom and a car parked in the driveway. Normally, houses on both sides are deserted after Labor Day."

As Tuesday night wore on, the low pressure gained ground and sent a cold front straight into Hurricane Grace, and overnight, the Nor'easter consumed Grace, taking the hurricane's energy and adding to its own as it slowly moved west toward the coast. Meanwhile, those on shore tried to move on with their normal lives while still keeping an eye on the storm. For Bernier, this meant dealing with those she saw in her work as a psychologist, but needless to say, many of them were feeling more stress than usual. "On Wednesdays I work in my home doing therapy with clients. My first appointment was at 9:00 a.m. and I began to work as if this day were like any other. In the back of my mind I had ascertained that because I had sat through the 4:15 a.m. tide when it was dark, the daylight of the 4:30 p.m. tide would be less scary. Low tide was about 10:00 a.m. and I remember noticing then that the sea had receded very little, if at all. Water was still at the seawall where normally low tide would reveal 100 yards of sandy beach beyond the seawall. About noon time, as I was sitting with a client in the first floor room I used for an office, there was a rushing sound coming from just outside the room. Although we were startled, I knew what it was, having watched and listened to it during the night, and I laughingly said 'oh, it's only the tide coming in!' I took her to the window. The scene was a torrent of water rushing down the stairs outside our door and pouring out onto the yard and street beyond."

Satellite image of the storm hitting the Northeast on October 30

By the time she had finished lunch, Bernier knew that she needed to rethink her plans for the rest of the day: "I returned two telephone calls that had come in on my answering machine while I was meeting with clients. I told both people of the action of the sea that I was witnessing outside my home. Incredibly, I had no sense of alarm, no hint of the danger advancing on me. I have since learned the waves were 35 feet high, explaining why I couldn't see any dark water troughs between white caps! I remember now making another call to a year round neighbor to check out her perceptions of the situation. I got an answering machine. As I prepared a salad for lunch, I noted the increasing depth of the water flooding the street. Because there were still two hours left before the next high tide I decided the water would probably not recede in time for my 6:30 p.m. client to get into the street. I decided to cancel that appointment. I picked up the telephone — but the line was dead. I went downstairs to the office to try another phone line. The second line worked and I placed the call."

Bernier was almost unable to finish her call because the adverse weather demanded immediate attention: "As I explained to the client why I had to cancel, the sea suddenly came flooding in the back door to the room where I was standing. Simultaneously, I heard weird noises and instantly knew (and told the client), 'I've got to get out of here!' The sounds I heard were a booming noise to my right and sharper crashing noise to my left. Slamming the phone down, I ran up the stairs, grabbed my jacket and purse. The water was too deep to get my car out of the street. I ran back down to the phone and called the police, asking them to come and get me. They said they would try. Feeling the immediacy of the situation, I decided to wait outside. I left the house through the garage as the crashing noises had been near the main door and I didn't want to get hit by flying timbers. When I saw for the first time what the situation looked like from outside, I jumped into the back seat of my car for safety to await the police."

Chapter 4: Sudden and Violent Nature

Pictures of flooding in Ocean City, New Jersey

"The desire to know what happened has not abated. I ask other survivors to tell me their stories. I particularly want to know the time sequence in their stories. I cling to the insights and explanations offered to me by the Storm Aid outreach worker whose skill and compassion have been significant instruments of healing for me. I still struggle to fathom what seems beyond my grasp ... beyond my ability to comprehend. The sudden and violent nature of this life-threatening disaster that destroyed most of my household belongings (accumulated over 30 years) and partially destroyed the home I was living in, will remain incomprehensible to me. My struggle to know and understand what happened represents a very basic human need to try to control for, as much as is possible, what is ultimately uncontrollable." - Elizabeth Bernier

While Bernier waited for the police, others up and down the coast were learning that there was no place that was truly safe except farther inland, away from the seas and the wind. The problem was that no one had expected or prepared for the storm to get this bad, so individuals and officials alike were caught off guard. For people like Bernier, that meant finding a new way to help themselves instead on counting on others for help. She explained, "In a matter of seconds, I knew it wasn't safe even there. Quickly, I left the car and began to make my way out of the street towards higher ground. The icy water was rushing in torrents from my right, pouring over the seawall, coming between each house, sweeping toward and past me. Moving against the powerful current, I held onto picket fence posts as I made my way very carefully. I was very conscious of not wanting to fall and placed my feet deliberately to remain sure-footed. The water in some areas was up to mid-thigh, in others about mid-calf. Although I have no recall of the winds, I later learned that they were ferocious, gusting to 70 and 80 mph. My concentration must have been so focused on getting through the water without falling, that I couldn't afford to notice the wind. That seems incredible to me now."

Obviously, Bernier was not the only one now in danger, even if others were slower to realize it. In fact, she noticed that she was far from alone in her situation as the sea continued to rise, flooding the area with a dangerous surge of water. It was not like a flood brought on by rain, where the water slowly rises and one has a chance to escape, but violent, dangerous and quick. "At some point I crossed the street, heading away from the ocean, in hopes that the water was shallower on the other side. Some teenage boys were behind me as I started out of the street. Initially they were laughing and making jokes. However, before too many minutes had passed their tone turned serious as they realized the rapidly escalating danger in the situation. From the direction I was heading, a truck came toward me. As it came alongside of me, it turned around and I thought the driver was going to pick me up. When the truck turned however, I remember seeing that the cab was filled with what looked like a generator. The driver then turned back away from the rapidly flooding street. As I approached what seemed to be even deeper water, I could see higher ground up ahead. I had to cross a driveway that pitched downward from the street toward the pond behind the houses. Thinking the water would be shallow, the teenage boys made their way down to the end of the driveway. As I watched them, I could tell the water got deeper at the end of the driveway so I started to cross about mid-point. Even here, the water came close to my hips. A man came out of the house and yelled I guess I better get out of here!' He followed me, as did the boys."

Finally, just as she was beginning to wonder if she had made a mistake in abandoning her car, Bernier began to reach a place of safety: "Gradually, the ground began to rise and water became shallower. I knew then that I was safe. I kept walking toward the end of the street looking for a phone to call the police to report my safety. Finally, I found a house with someone home and used the phone. The police told me they had attempted to get in to help me in a 4-wheel drive vehicle but were unable to make it through the water. I then called friends and asked them to pick me up. We agreed to meet a few short blocks away at a major intersection back from the ocean. I had to make my way through backyards to get to dry ground as the ocean was pouring up the adjacent street. Waiting for my friends, I saw cars filling the two main streets creating a traffic jam at the intersection. I recall wanting to shout to the drivers, 'No! No! Don't go down there to look — you don't know how dangerous it is!!' As a police cruiser arrived and the policeman began to direct traffic away from the street, I started to become aware of just how wet and cold I was as I waited for my ride."

Fortunately, Bernier didn't have to wait for long, as she would soon be out of the storm, at least physically. That said, a sense of emotional safety would have to wait. "When my friends arrived, we drove a few blocks north and up a hill to check on property they owned and rented in the neighborhood. As one friend checked the house, the other friend and I walked through backyards to see the ocean. Looking down the coast, I could see my house, the waves crashing against it. We left there and drove south on a road parallel to my street. As we approached the back side of the pond, I asked them to park so I could look across and check once again on what was happening to my house. I watched as a huge wave hit and suddenly my house disappeared! All I could see was water crashing over where the house should have been. Quickly, the water receded and I saw the house was still standing. Suddenly, it was gone again as the next wave hit, obliterating it from view. I felt frozen with terror. I watched as wave after wave engulfed the house that I had been in less than an hour ago. There was yet an hour to go before the height of the tide. I couldn't believe my eyes. I couldn't believe that I had been in that house just minutes before with no thought of leaving, no awareness of the growing danger. That scene stays in my mind and I still feel the tears surface in me when I tell about it. The terror and the disbelief still seize me. Later, I would identify with the Biblical story of Lot's wife. I understood then that she had been immobilized with terror when she looked back — having been driven from, yet trying to stay connected with, her home, only to witness its destruction and that of her community."

For Bernier, the psychological impact of the storm proved to be much worse than the physical impact would ever be. Even after she was safe, she could not shake the stone cold terror in her heart. "My friends took me to their home where I exchanged my cold, wet clothing for a warm robe and sat before the wood stove feeling numb. As the time of high tide approached I was filled with a passionate desire to know what was happening at the coast. I felt glued to the TV watching for every news account I could find. I read every newspaper story I could find, then and since."

Chapter 5: Combination of High Tides, Gale-Force Winds and Storm-Driven

"An unusual and powerful combination of high tides, gale-force winds and storm-driven waves flooded low-lying coastal areas from the Carolinas to Maine last night, washing away houses on Long Island and capsizing boats off Connecticut. An Air National Guard rescue helicopter with five people aboard was reported down in the water and missing. Meteorologists said they expected the storm to 'keep on howling' through most of today and tonight as it follows its westward course toward the mainland, making for a soggy Halloween. ... The helicopter, with five crew members aboard, was reported missing late last night in the stormy waters some 60 miles south of Long Island. The helicopter went into the water at about 9:45 P.M., said Chief Petty Officer Alan Burd, a spokesman for the Coast Guard at Westhampton. He said the helicopter was returning to the Suffolk County Air National Guard Base in Westhampton after an unsuccessful attempt to rescue a man adrift on a sailboat some 210 miles south of Nantucket." - John T. McQuiston in "Storm Batters Shore; 5 Missing on Rescue Copter," October 31, 1991

While people living along the shore were dealing with the storm and trying to escape its wrath, some in the air were actually heading towards it. Major David Ruvola was in an Air National Guard H-60 helicopter, and along with his co-pilot, Captain Graham Buschor, he was flying into the eye of the storm to look for a man who had fallen off a Romanian freighter. With him were Jim Mioli and PJs (parachute jumpers) John Spillane and Rick Smith. In spite of their best efforts, the weather was too bad for them to function in and they had to give up hopes of finding the missing man. Ruvola explained, "We were looking down at 30- to 40-foot seas and the winds were 40 to 50 knots. We didn't know whether or not a PJ dropped into the water would be able to make it onto the boat, and whether or not we'd be able to get him back off the boat. The hoist operator was concerned that — because of the size of the wave-swells — the cable could be snapped while hoisting someone back into the helicopter. All considered, we decided to allow the C-130 that was overhead to drop survival gear [to the stranded sailor] and head for home."

While the sailor they were looking for was eventually rescued by someone else, Ruvola and his men were not so lucky. At 8:00 that evening, Ruvola tried to connect with a C-130 sent to refuel him. Refueling in the air is tricky business under the best of circumstances, and during this storm, it was nearly impossible. Ruvola recalled, "It was very, very turbulent and we were trying to find smoother air to complete the final refueling. We continued to climb and even descend below the clouds. At one point, we were 500 feet above the water and you could see the ragged, bottom edge of the clouds mixing on the horizon with the whitewater of the ocean."

After trying for more than an hour to complete the refueling move, Ruvola ran out of time and was forced to ditch the helicopter in the raging Atlantic. At his command, Buschor sent a desperate mayday out to the *Tamaroa*, a Coast Guard cutter just a few miles away. He later explained, "I remember very vividly my call for help. I was painting the *Tamaroa* on our radar, so I knew it was only 12 miles away. Unfortunately, we didn't have enough fuel to go that far. The *Tamaroa* responded almost immediately and told us to head toward them. We knew the number one engine was about to roll off-line because of fuel starvation. I remember telling the *Tamaroa*, 'Negative, negative, we are ditching right here!'"

The Tamaroa

At that point, Ruvola and his men prepared to jump out of trouble in the air and into trouble in the water. On his command, Buschor, Smith and Spillane bailed out, and Buschor subsequently described the scene: "The wind was kicking up salt spray, the landing lights were making everything hazy and beyond that it was pitch black, so really I couldn't see anything at first. Fortunately, my night-vision goggles were still attached to my helmet. I wasn't willing to jump without being able to see, so I flipped the goggles back over my eyes, took a deep breath and jumped off the footboard. ... In the military you train to the point that it gets boring and monotonous, but what's amazing is that when you get into a stressful situation, you respond the way you were trained. It's almost like you're on automatic and you don't have to think about what to do next. Once I hit the water, the first thing that entered my mind was to consolidate survival gear and look for other survivors. That's when it became apparent I was going to be doing that the rest of the evening."

With three of his men safely out, Ruvola and Mioli rode the crippled H-60 into the sea, but they landed upside down in the black night and immediately began fighting to escape the quickly sinking helicopter. Ruvola remembered, "You're trained in dunker training to always maintain a hand-hold in underwater situations like that. With that hand-hold you know pretty much where you are in relation to the exits on the helicopter. My primary exit was the pilot-door next to me. I grabbed the handle, turned it and the door opened, thank God."

As soon as he was out of the chopper, Ruvola activated his survival vest, which quickly propelled him to the water's surface. There he found Mioli, who was freezing in the frigid water. Hoping to help his friend survive, Ruvola "took my wet-suit hood from my pocket and put it on Jim's head to help keep him warm." The two men then found Spillane, who had several broken ribs, a broken leg, and a shattered arm, as well as some internal injuries.

Fortunately, the *Tamaroa* was on its way. According to a citation of commendation the crew later received, "While pounding north through the relentless seas, *TAMAROA* was diverted to assist an Air National Guard HH-60 helicopter which had been forced to ditch at sea, due to fuel exhaustion, some 90 nautical miles south of Montauk, New York. With the seas now in excess of 40 feet and winds gusting more than 80 knots, *TAMAROA* steamed the 15 miles in five hours. HU-25 CG2116, already on scene, sighted four men in the water fighting for their lives in the mountainous waves. CG1493 tried for 43 minutes to recover the four survivors, but the rescue basked simply blew straight back in the 60 to 70 knot winds. *TAMAROA* made eight approaches on the men for two hours as wave after wave crashed over the ship. The first man was brought aboard using scramble nets, eventually the other three were rescued in the same manner. *TAMAROA*'s use of the winds and seas to recover the four men was an extraordinary effort given the 50 degree rolls, the heavy seas and 60 plus knots of wind. The valiant rescue efforts pushed *TAMAROA*, its crew and the air crews to the limits of endurance. The professionalism and devotion to duty exhibited by *TAMAROA* are in keeping with the highest traditions of the United States Coast Guard."

About four and a half hours later, the *Tamaroa* rescued Buschor, who remembered, "I couldn't believe I was on the deck of the Coast Guard cutter. I didn't think I was going to make it, and it was almost an overpowering sensation that I had made it that far. The guys immediately picked me up and threw me inside, cut my clothes off and wrapped me in blankets. I was pleading for something to drink, but they wouldn't give me anything because they were afraid I might have internal injuries."

Another 40 minutes passed before the crew found Ruvola, Spillane and Mioli, but sadly, Rick Smith was never seen again. Buschor praised his comrade and remarked on the irony that the one crew member lost at sea was one trained to rescue others in a similar predicament: "Rick was a great guy with a very quiet demeanor — a true professional. He knew his stuff. Losing him was very hard. What I couldn't fathom was that he was a PJ, yet I made it out alive and he didn't. It is extremely difficult to accept the loss."

Chapter 6: The Damaging Winds

"The damaging winds came sweeping out of a clear sky, taking many along the shoreline by surprise. While the gusts were short of hurricane force, they were bearing straight in on the coast in an unusual conjunction that in effect forced water ashore, said Mr. McElhearn. 'This type of storm happens rarely,' he said. 'The direction is normally west to east.' While for inland areas last night was a clear, crisp extension of a beautiful fall day, many residents of coastal towns on Long Island and in southern New Jersey found themselves coping with emergency bulletins or contemplating evacuation. The storm was first felt on eastern Long Island yesterday afternoon. Its first licks washed away five unoccupied houses along Dune Road in Westhampton. By 7 P.M., it had flooded the White Horse and Black Horse Pikes into Atlantic City and capsized three boats in Long Island Sound off the Connecticut coast. Ten people were rescued from the boats. In Seabright, N.J., the police early today were awaiting the arrival of a National Guard unit to assist in the evacuation of any residents who wanted to leave their homes, said Sgt. Steve Spahr. High tides had flooded the town's main street, he said. In the Sea Gate section of Brooklyn, residents living near the Narrows piled sandbags last night against tides running five feet above normal. Homes in a two-block area were evacuated." - John McQuiston

By Thursday morning, October 31, the storm had reached its peak, and it was also on this day that Bob Case, who was with the National Weather Service, inadvertently gave the disaster its most popular name. He explained, "It was an unprecedented set of circumstances. A strong disturbance associated with a cold front moved along the U.S.-Canadian border on October 27 and passed through New England pretty much without incident. At the same time, a huge high pressure system was forecast to build over southeast Canada. When a low pressure system along the front moved into the Maritimes southeast of Nova Scotia, it began to intensify due to the cold dry air introduced from the north. These circumstances alone, could have created a strong storm. But then, like throwing gasoline on a fire, a dying hurricane Grace delivered immeasurable tropical energy to create the perfect storm. With all of the contributing factors coming together at just the right time, in less than 24 hours, the storm exploded to epic proportions and then headed toward the coast. If any of the components were out of sync, the epic storm would not have happened." In fact, Case's description became the closest thing to an official name that the unusual storm would ever have, as it developed too quickly for meteorologists to actually christen it anything. During the years that followed, it was referred to by some weathermen as the "No-Name Storm."

Sometime around 2:00 that morning, the authorities ordered the shoreline along much of New York and New England evacuated. Christopher Hartney of Ventnor, New Jersey told one reporter, "The bay is already in my yard and it's a couple of feet deep in the street. It's ironic, because it's not raining. But then again, it's just water and I can swim. I just didn't expect to do it in my own back yard."

During that night, a number of people had to be rescued as they had gotten caught on boats out in the storm. Among those pulled from the surging waters that night was Ray Leonard, who was aboard the *Satori*. While the two women sailing with him, Karen Stimson and Susan Bylander, later expressed fear that their boat might not survive the night, Leonard was initially unconcerned. He admitted, "I'd guess the seas were 15 to 18 feet, tops. Satori had been in much worse. It was a very uncomfortable ride, but the boat was sound and we weren't taking on water, except for a few gallons that came through the hatch. ... You never head towards shore in a heavy storm. It's too dangerous. And the weather forecast said a hurricane was heading towards Bermuda, so it didn't make sense to keep going that way. When I knew the crew would have to jump in the water, I wasn't comfortable about having them go alone. Also, I knew if I disobeyed I wouldn't be able to land in a U.S. port for several years, and I've seen expatriates in foreign ports. I didn't want to be one."

However, the Coast Guard had a very different version of events that evening. According to a citation of commendation that those who rescued Leonard received, "USCGC *TAMAROA* (WMEC 166) encountered seas up to 30 feet and winds in excess of 50 knots while responding to a distress onboard the sailing vessel SATORI. HH-3F CG1493 (a helicopter) was unable to hoist the three people and took up station and watched as *TAMAROA* launched its own rescue effort. *TAMAROA*'s Rigid Hull Inflatable (RHI), damaged by the severe sea conditions during the launch was able to pass mustang suits to the SATORI crew. When SATORI's bow came crashing down on the RHI, the small boat rescue was no longer possible. SATORI's crew was led to the water and hoisted by CG1493."

Shawn Sullivan was a member of the *Tamaroa*'s crew that day and remembered, "It's probably a good thing we didn't because of how awful it was. ... I remember standing on deck and looking up looking at a mountain of water and not being able to see the top of the water. And every time, we would just chug our way up. ... I'll never forget the sound. I imagine it's similar to how people describe tornados. It was an unbelievable noise, ripping through wires and antennas, making these god-awful screams. ... There's no doubt, somewhere in the back of my mind I thought if I'm going to go out, why not go out doing something as heroic as this. ... It was probably the greatest rescues any of us were a part of. For sure, all of us on that ship look back and say 'man there's no way we should have come home.' ... [The *Tamaroa* is] not just iron. She's not just metal. She's seen more than most of us have seen in our lives."

Over the decades that followed, Leonard maintained that he had had no need for help, and more than 20 years later, he asserted, "We were well able and braced for a storm such as that, the perfect storm. I think we were in MUCH better shape than the Coast Guard." In fact, he added that anyone facing a coming storm should be well-prepared and ready to go it alone: "A storm...like the perfect storm, whatever that was — people tend to think that, 'Someone will come help me. Someone will come take care of me.' In other words, they don't look to be self-sufficient. ...Because if this does hit, you're going to lose all those little things you've spent the last 20 years feeling good about. Living on a boat is one thing during a disaster. But living in a house in a city is a different thing completely."

While the Coast Guard viewed the rescue as necessary, Leonard's faith in his boat may have been well-founded, because the *Satori* eventually washed up on the coast of Maryland. At that time, he recalled, "A park ranger found my phone number in it. He called me up and said come get your boat. It was fine. I went down and had her hauled off, cleaned her up, then sailed her to Florida. … Bluewater sailors are sharp, self-reliant, and proud."

Chapter 7: Wreckage of Homes and Eroded Beaches

"Disaster relief officials, environmental experts and grim property owners surveyed the wreckage of homes and eroded beaches along wave-battered coasts from New England to the mid-Atlantic states yesterday as estimates of last week's storm damage climbed into the hundreds of millions of dollars. At least four deaths were attributed to the storm, which howled and hit like a hurricane and then moved slowly down the coast on Tuesday, Wednesday and Thursday. The storm reduced coastal homes to kindling and tossed ships and boats like toys, endangering scores of people at sea. A sea-and-air search went on for a third day for a missing Air National Guard rescue specialist whose helicopter ditched 60 miles south of Long Island on Wednesday night. But the focus of the search shifted to Virginia coastal areas. The missing man was believed to be drifting 100 miles a day." Robert McFadden in "REPORT ON DAMAGE IN STORM IS GRIM," November 3, 1991

By the time the storm ended, it had left behind a shocking amount of destruction, some of which was described by Elizabeth Bernier: "Thursday morning, the day after the storm, one of my friends took me back to my home to see what had happened. We were unable to get into the street by car. The scene reminded me of pictures of Desert Storm damage to Iraq and Kuwait. Piles of rocks, broken slabs of concrete, piles of sand, broken furniture, timbers, automobiles; in short, rubble blocked the street. We climbed over and around, down the road to my house. At one point, a woman with a professional camera on her shoulder came climbing out, passing us. Her face reflected the horror she had seen. I asked 'What is it?' She shook her head and said 'It's all gone — all gone!' My heart sank. We approached my house and I saw my car up on the lawn between the garage and the street. It had been swept from its place in the driveway. The entrance door to the house was blown into the hallway and, as I approached I could see the chaos within."

As Bernier continued to approach the place she had once called home, her shock only grew as she took in more of the scene. "I climbed up to the front of the house via my neighbor's concrete ramp, which was located near the seawall but had somehow remained intact. What I saw now looked exactly like a bombed out city in war-time. Gaping black holes across the whole front of my house on both stories where sliding glass doors and windows had been, porches gone, the balcony ripped off and hanging at a bizarre angle outside my bedroom. The entire concrete apron between the house and seawall ripped out exposing deep craters filled with rocks and debris. My neighbor's house — the entire front one third completely ripped out — the same or worse scene repeated, as I looked down the coast and then behind me as I turned to look in the other direction — the same devastation. I didn't want to see anymore; but I knew I had to go inside. We entered the house through the gaping holes to find everything smashed. The powerful, raging sea, driven by hurricane force winds had smashed into, broken open and at places, driven through my home, leaving piled up in the far corners the rubble of broken furniture, seaweed, glass, sand, books, tapes, food, papers, dishes, baby pictures (8 mm films), family antiques, jewelry, bedding, records, lamps, appliances, music, clothing, plants .... everything I owned! The sea took some of it out the side doors into the street and beyond to the fenced edge of the pond. It took other things out with the receding tide, never to be found. I felt stunned. Later, I would feel ravaged."

Obviously, Bernier was only one of many experiencing a similar sense of horror at what they were seeing, but her words captured the emotions that many others doubtless felt: "As I made my way through the house, I found the destruction of the first two floors so massive that I again became terrified to think that I was nearly trapped in this destruction. Had I not left when I did, there would have been no safe place for me. After carefully inspecting the stairs for safety, I climbed to the third floor; the damage left holes in walls, shifting door frames, etc. I found the front half of the house, especially my bedroom, reduced to rubble. The back two bedrooms were dry and untouched. Looking at them, I knew I never could have conceived of safety being on the top floor in the back bedrooms. I had to flee from there during the night because I thought the smashing waves were tearing the house off the foundation. Climbing higher appeared much too risky to me. For days and weeks afterward I was obsessed with the thought of where I would have gone in that house. I would have been trapped — I would have gone mad! I kept trying to figure out what I might have done to keep safe, physically and mentally. Finally, my mind uncovered a semi-safe corner, on top of the kitchen counter, out of the 'line of fire' of the raging waves and flying debris. Later, when I read a newspaper account of an 80 year old woman in Scituate who sat out the storm playing solitaire in her kitchen, I knew I would likely have done the same. Solitaire is a very centering activity for me that I use often."

Of course, while the storm on land was winding down, those at sea still faced at great deal of danger. Willi Bank was the engineer on the old schooner *Ernestina* when it left New England for Bermuda that week, and as he later put it, "We were running away from Hurricane Grace. When things got better there, we were told about the other storm. I said, 'What do you mean there's a more severe storm out there?'" Willi's father, William, added, "We were in terrific seas, but nothing as bad as the people who perished." Nonetheless, the crew suffered terrible anguish as they listened helplessly to other vessels founder and go down. Gregg Swanzey, the captain of the *Ernestina*, said, "We knew people on board. The captain [of the Anna Christina) had sailed as a mate on the Ernestina. All we could do was just listen. It was awful to hear." Fortunately, the Coast Guard was able to rescue the crew of the Anne Christina, though not without grave danger to their own lives.

Like so many, Greg Machos had his own story to tell after he was able to evacuate his home in New Jersey and observe the event from a safe distance: "My personal recollections of the Halloween Storm were the news reports of what was occurring along the Jersey Shore and Long

Island, where there was tidal flooding. That year there were several coastal storms: Hurricane Bob, which went east of Long Island, and into New England back in August, this storm, and then a Nor'easter in December, 1991. I didn't realize until many years later that Hurricane Grace was a component of the Halloween storm. There wasn't a whole lot of media coverage of hurricanes in October unless you followed the Weather Channel, and by late October, Tropical Updates that were seen every day during the peak season, were no longer featured since the transition was taking place between summer and winter, and more focus was being made on winter storms. In light of what has happened in recent years, that has changed to some extent. ...the Perfect Storm didn't cause as much damage along the Jersey coast, or Long Island as much as it did in New England. News footage from the movie adaptation of the book, The Perfect Storm, written by Sebastian Junger, showed tremendous waves pounding the shoreline. Nevertheless, I do recall my older brother saying how the storm produced much stronger winds than Hurricane Bob did here in Central Jersey. ... In the case of the Halloween storm, New Jersey felt the effects of a frontal boundary that was passing through, and the pressure gradient created between the combined low pressure off the coast and the high pressure building in behind the front."

Chapter 8: An Intense Atlantic Storm

"An intense Atlantic storm dubbed E.T. built surging tides that hurled 20-foot waves into low-lying East Coast areas Thursday, ravaging houses, boats, sea defenses and beaches from Maine to Florida. ... More than 100 beachfront homes in Maine, including President Bush's vacation home at Kennebunkport were damaged. The stone pier where Bush docks his speedboat Fidelity outside his house was ripped with a 15- to 20-foot hole. ... At least one death was blamed on the Atlantic storm. Two people were reported missing, a fisherman who was swept from a rocky point at Narrragansett, R.I., on Tuesday night, and an Air National Guardsman whose four crewmate were rescued from a life raft early Thursday after their helicopter went down. The 200-mile-wide Atlantic storm formed earlier this week of Canada and is called "extra-tropical" because it didn't originate in the tropics as hurricanes do. ... At high tide Thursday morning, waves up to 20 feet crashed against Boston Light, a lighthouse. It pushed rivers through inland back yards and commuter routes, punched holes in wooden seawalls and smashed others to pieces, flooded coastal towns and collapsed houses, knocked out power to thousands. It tossed boats onto shore, eroded beaches as far south as Palm Beach, Florida, and prompted dozens of seas rescues." - John McQuiston

The Perfect Storm had wreaked all kinds of havoc over the past several days, but it still wasn't done by the time Halloween was over. In fact, it was still moving towards the East Coast as November came, and people living in the Northeast still had to brace for more. Governor John R. McKernan of Maine declared a state of emergency on November 1: "This storm produced an unexpected amount of damage and flooding in southern coastal areas. While Maine did not suffer the very widespread damage the storm inflicted on parts of southern New England and New York, reports clearly indicate that we have had substantial damage." A Maine police officer, Judy Stutes, elaborated on the kinds of damage she had seen: "There is some extensive damage. On a lot of them, foundations are gone, and the insides of the homes are all washed out. We've had a lot of sand and debris and rocks from the ocean washed into people's front yards and in their basements. I know a couple of homes had a couple of feet of sand in their basements or living rooms. We've been out all day cleaning up the sand off the roadways and inspecting damages."

Finally, on November 2, the storm actually made landfall, with the eye crossing over Nova Scotia. The storm may have been a unique and unlucky convergence of multiple storms, but like any other storm beginning at sea, it began to weaken once it no longer had water to feed on. Nevertheless, it left behind a wide strip of damage that affected rich and poor alike. Among those who suffered property damage was President George H. W. Bush. Speaking of President Bush's vacation home a Kennebunkport, Maine, Marlin Fitzwater told the press, "There is extraordinary damage inside the home and the other buildings…there are reports of windows and walls being caved in and a disastrous situation there with regard to their personal property. …the back porch of the house is now located down by the (Secret Service) command post."

Satellite image of the unnamed hurricane on November 2

President Bush finally got to see his home on November 2, when he took a group of reporters on a tour of the damage. In the process, he told them, "Unfortunately, the sea won this round. ... There's always tomorrow. ... It's our family strength, being this close to the ocean, We'll figure it out. ... These guys who live here all the time have never seen anything like it, ever...We're talking about hundred-year storms." Standing by her husband's side, Barbara Bush refused to despair, saying "It was devastating. But life goes on. And you know, a lot of people's homes were hurt. But all the way up and down the east coast. And we had another home, the White House, temporarily, and so we could survive. A lot of people had a lot more trouble than we did."

One of the people along with the president described the visit with more details: "I was with President Bush when he returned to Kennebunkport after the nor'easter storm in November 1991. And the whole first floor of the house was destroyed. ... Water came in one side and out the other side. It took everything with. ... All of the personal mementoes and photographs and autograph books were all strewn in the Bushes and valuable personal treasures scattered over the lawn. There was a foot and a half of rock on the tennis court. ... They were picking up pieces of photographs and keepsakes that they had. And he would say hey, Barbara, look at this. And she would say George, come over here and take a look at this. And you could see that it was just a terrible shock for them. But at the same time, you saw strength in both of them. ... My first reaction was how sad it was for my parents. And of course, both of them, being so optimistic, they were like don't worry about it. Everything is going to be fine. ... He didn't even flinch. He looked at that devastation and the president of the United States put on a pair of rubber coat coveralls and immediately started shoveling sand out of his living room. ... He was pretty depressed. But he also said, we're going to put it back together. We're going to fix it. This is still going to be my favorite place and I'm going to come back here. That perfect storm defined what he felt had happened in his life that year."

In the end, the long-term damage along the East Coast proved to be much worse than anyone might have predicted. According to one report filed in early November, "From Maine to Virginia, officials said, hundreds of shore-front houses were destroyed by the storm and thousands of other homes ... heavily damaged by floodwaters and winds. Many of the homes were among the most expensive in the area. Environmental experts said hundreds of miles of fragile dunes and sandy beaches had been gouged away by 25-foot waves and winds just short of 74-mile-an-hour hurricane force. In many shore areas of Cape Cod, Long Island and New Jersey and on barrier islands like Fire Island and the Outer Banks of North Carolina, cliffs jutted up where pristine beaches had been. ... The Governors of New York, New Jersey, Massachusetts and Maine said they would appeal for Federal disaster aid for stricken areas after the destruction is fully assessed. Such aid includes low-interest loans to individuals and small businesses and money for states and cities to repair roads, bridges and other public structures. ...the storm last week left wreckage almost entirely along coastal areas, with people and property untouched only a short way inland. Estimates of the damage are preliminary and are likely to rise, officials said, and in the case of lost dunes and beaches the destruction is not easy to assess. Hundreds of millions of dollars spent on erosion-control projects on Long Island beaches may have been lost, environmental experts said. Gov. William F. Weld of Massachusetts estimated that property damage in his state alone would reach 'hundreds of millions of dollars'..."

As is always the case in a natural disaster, the American Red Cross was among the first on the scene to offer help. The report continued, "The American Red Cross in Boston said 3,000 homes on the shores of Cape Cod and Massachusetts Bay had been damaged sufficiently to force their residents to evacuate. Anne Wilcox, a Red Cross spokeswoman, said that 584 houses had major damage and that 172 had been swept away or reduced to rubble. 'And these are just preliminary estimates,' she said."

Chapter 9: Chewing Away More of the Beach with Each High Tide

"With luck, geologists say, most of the damaged beaches along the storm's path from Maine south will recover to some extent, though few will return to their original condition without multimillion-dollar sand replenishment projects. But others, especially fragile barrier islands…may not survive. A lot depends on the weather this winter, the season when northeasters like the one that struck last week bear down on the coast. While hurricanes get the bad press, northeasters are the storms that, year in and year out, do the most damage to the coast. These storms disturb the beach's 'equilibrium profile,' a sort of resting position each beach adopts depending on its sand grain size, prevailing wave pattern and other factors. The profile is maintained in summer, when swells roll in, pick up sand and deposit it on the beach. … When these waves break on the beach, their energy is dissipated as water seeps into the sand, but the beach cannot dissipate the high energy of the quick, steep waves of a northeaster. They create heavy backwash and disturb the bottom, allowing sand to be carried away, said Dr. Orrin H. Pilkey, a professor of geology at Duke University. Also, water carried over land by the storm surge carries sediment away as it flows back out to sea. The effects are worsened because northeasters, unlike hurricanes that normally move rapidly across the shore, can hang around for days, chewing away more of the beach with each high tide." - Cory Dean

The Perfect Storm took a horrific toll on human life and personal property, but the storm's longest lasting effect was what it did to the coastline, especially the beaches in the Northeastern United States. Kenneth H. Jones of Long Island observed, "I was here for all the hurricanes and everything since 1970, There's never been anything like this. Never. … This used to be a 12- to 16-foot dune. The storm leveled it right off." Dr. Stephen Leatherman agreed, saying, "The first high tide takes the beach away, and the second starts hitting the dunes and the third moves into the buildings. In a northeaster, steep waves are coming in very quickly The beach is submerged. It is always wet. So it's easier to move the sand…There will be some recovery in a week or so. But probably 50 percent or so will stay on the bars and some of it was pushed beyond the bars, and that won't come back. … We won't know how much comes back until July or August after we have a couple of months of heavy swells. … Replenishment is a lost cause there. Things have gone so far now I don't see how they can bring them back. This storm proves again that we're looking at an island almost down to its last sand grain."

As bad as the Perfect Storm was, it likely never would have been remembered by anyone west of the Mississippi had it not been for an injured tree surgeon named Sebastian Junger. He explained how he got into writing about the storm: "I was living in Gloucester in 1991. I was working as a climber for a tree company, taking trees down. This massive storm hit the coast and really destroyed a lot of the Massachusetts coast. What I saw in Gloucester was overwhelming… the violence of the storm was just overwhelming. I later found out that a Gloucester sword fishing boat had gone down. The Andrea Gail had gone down five hundred miles off shore. They were coming back from a one month trip to the Grand Banks. I was thinking about writing a book on dangerous jobs. I had hurt myself pretty badly doing tree work and it got me thinking that people don't pay much attention to jobs that are really dangerous... it would be interesting to write a book about that. So, originally I was going to write a chapter on the Andrea Gail. She went down in an area of one hundred foot seas. It was one of the biggest storms ever recorded off the east coast. Eventually that chapter turned into a whole book."

While Junger's subsequent book, *The Perfect Storm*, was considered by people who lived through the devastation to be a mostly accurate and objective presentation of events, the movie by the same name was not as popular with those who made their living in the fishing trade. In fact, some of those mentioned and their families were so offended that they eventually filed a lawsuit against Warner Brothers, the company that produced the movie, claiming, "Unlike the book, the Picture presented a concededly dramatized account of both the storm and the crew of the Andrea Gail. For example, the main protagonist in the Picture, Billy Tyne, was portrayed as a down-and-out sword boat captain who was obsessed with the next big catch. In one scene, the Picture relates an admittedly fabricated depiction of Tyne berating his crew for wanting to return to port in Gloucester, Massachusetts. Warner Bros. took additional liberties with the land-based interpersonal relationships between the crewmembers and their families. While the Picture did not hold itself out as factually accurate, it did indicate at the beginning of the film that 'THIS FILM IS BASED ON A TRUE STORY.' A disclaimer inserted during the closing credits elaborated on this point with the following statement: 'This film is based on actual historical events contained in `The Perfect Storm' by Sebastian Junger. Dialogue and certain events and characters in the film were created for the purpose of fictionalization.'" The lawsuit was eventually thrown out of court, but the grieving families never forgave those whom they felt had maligned the names of their loved ones.

The popular movie undoubtedly dramatized the events, and while it did depict Linda Greenlaw, it did not cover the actions she took in the wake of the storm. In fact, Greenlaw went searching one last time for the crew of the *Andrea Gail* after everyone else had given up, and she wrote about her futile search: "As we approached the Sable Island area from the east, bound for home, Bob Brown asked that we pass the island closer and slower than usual, taking time to look for some sign of the Andrea Gail. She was one week overdue in her homecoming, and the Canadian Coast Guard had found evidence that she might have experienced some trouble in the area surrounding Sable Island. There wasn't a breath of wind that day, and the fog was so thick it collected in cold drops that clung to our eyebrows and lashes. We couldn't see 100 feet from the boat. But still we looked. We searched in the fog all day, hoping to stumble into the scene that played on the reel-to-reel in my head. My mind's eye saw a raft, which, when we got closer, we could see held the six fishermen from the Andrea Gail, all smiling and waving. Like a mirage in a desert, the fog can play tricks with your eyes and mind, showing you whatever you want to see if you look hard enough. We had been squinting into the fog over the bow for hours when something white appeared in the water ahead of us. It didn't disappear when I blinked. It was real."

For a brief moment, hope soared upon the sight of the object, but it merely proved to be one more piece of the heartbreaking puzzle. Greenlaw explained, "A plastic 55-gallon drum loomed eerily through the vapor. As we neared it, I maneuvered the boat so that the barrel floated slowly down the starboard rail, where the crew pulled it aboard. It was marked clearly with the letters "A.G.," and was not what I had hoped to find. The presence of the barrel from the Andrea Gail on our deck brought with it feelings of doom and hopelessness, and I was tempted to throw it back overboard. The Coast Guard had canceled its search by the time we arrived in Gloucester three days later, and by then any shred of hope that anyone still clung to rested with my crew and myself. We had no good news for the families and friends of the men lost with the Andrea Gail. In fact, we had only the empty barrel, a small piece of the puzzle. We didn't know anything that the Coast Guard hadn't already reported, and could give nobody reason to deny the fact that the boat and her six-man crew were gone forever."

Bibliography

Greenlaw, Linda. *The Hungry Ocean: A Swordboat Captain's Journey.* Hyperion. (2001)

Hoke, Jim (2005-02-16). "The Ocean Prediction Center and "The Perfect Storm"". *Oceanic Prediction Center*. National Oceanic and Atmospheric Administration.

Junger, Sebastian. *The Perfect Storm: A True Story of Men Against the Sea.* W. W. Norton and Company. (2009)

McCown, Sam (2008-08-20). ""Perfect Storm" Damage Summary". *National Climatic Data Center*. National Oceanic and Atmospheric Administration.

Pasch, Richard (1991). "Unnamed Hurricane Preliminary Report Page 4"

"Surviving The Perfect Storm - Air National Guard"

Made in the USA
Monee, IL
15 March 2021

62605257R00020